15 WAYS TO ZAP a BULLY!

JACKIE HUMANS, PhD

Legwork Team Publishing

ILLUSTRATIONS BY NIKKI LEE, AUTHOR'S DAUGHTER

Legwork Team Publishing
New York

Legwork Team Publishing
80 Davids Drive, Suite One
Hauppauge, NY 11788
www.legworkteam.com
Phone: 631-944-6511

Copyright © 2010 Jack-A-Bob, LLC

ISBN: 978-0-9843-5393-4 (sc)

First edition 2/2/2010

Printed in the United States of America
This book is printed on acid-free paper

Illustrations by Nikki Lee, author's daughter
Designed by Michelle Martinez

DEDICATION

This book is dedicated to the children of the world who get bullied,
and who feel powerless and alone.

ACKNOWLEDGMENTS

I would like to acknowledge the following people and organizations: Roz Piecka, my sister by birth and best friend by choice; my mother, Margaret Miller, one of the most courageous people I have ever known; my brother, Chris DeWalt, who knows a thing or two about redemption; and the original inspiration for this book, my daughter Nikki Lee.

I also want to acknowledge Child Abuse Prevention Services, a wonderful organization dedicated to helping children. Through my involvement, I have discovered how much I love empowering children.

Lastly, I'd like to acknowledge the author Elin McCoy. Many of the techniques mentioned inside came from her book, *What to Do When Kids Are Mean to Your Child*. Parents everywhere are strongly urged to run, not walk, to buy her book.

NOTE TO READERS

This book is not meant for dealing with physical bullying.
So, if a bully hits, pushes, kicks or hurts you physically
in any way, it should be reported to an adult right away.
It's not a good idea to fight back physically.
For one thing, that's usually not a good way
to solve any kind of problem and
for another thing, you could
end up getting really hurt.

Hi Kids,

Guess what? Everyone gets picked on by a bully at some time. This book shows you lots of ways to stop bullies in their tracks. Some are serious and some are silly, so just read through and see if you can find some that might work for you.

15 WAYS TO ZAP a BULLY!

#1 SPY ON THE BULLY

#2 CONCENTRATE ON COUNTING

#3 SILENTLY REPEAT FEEL-GOOD SENTENCE

#4 FOCUS ON THE POSITIVE

#5 LOOK BORED

#6 PRETEND TO BE THE BULLY'S BOSS

#7 CALL THE BULLY THE WRONG NAME

#8 OFFER TO HELP

#9 THANK THE BULLY

#10 YELL THE WORD "BULLY!"

#11 FAKE A FALL

#12 ASK IF THE BULLY'S FLIRTING

#13 TRAP THE BULLY WITH WORDS

#14 MAKE THE BULLY LOOK SILLY

#15 PUT IT IN WRITING

#1 SPY ON THE BULLY

Most bullies pick on kids who are by themselves. So, here's what you can do: start spying on the bully to see which other kids are getting picked on. These other kids can become your "bully-zapping" buddies, even if you only hang out with them while you're on the bus or on the playground or in the cafeteria. Bullies hate being outnumbered.

#10 YELL THE WORD "BULLY!"
Bullies like to strike when adults aren't around. You can get an adult's attention by yelling the word "bully" because nobody likes a bully.
"You think you're cool but you're just a BULLY!"

Another way to get an adult's attention is to try screaming as though you're in great pain.

Once an adult arrives, look embarrassed and say, "Oops, I guess my trick ankle gave out."

Then make sure to wink at the bully so he knows you can get him in trouble any time you want.

You can also ask bullies a sneaky question in order to trap them with words.

19

#14 MAKE THE BULLY LOOK SILLY

When a bully makes fun of something really obvious about you, like your height or weight, you can make them look silly instead.

"Kind of fat, aren't you?"

"WHO TOLD YOU?"

Keeping a journal of the times you've been bullied will help you be more believable. Remember to use the 5 W's: Who, What, Where, When and Witnesses. With a written record of the bullying, you will be able to give accurate information to an adult.

WITNESSES

Witnesses may be your most important "W" because they can back up your story. Just write in your journal who else saw the bullying happen. Later on, the teacher or principal can talk to these kids one at a time and get the whole story.

After writing down three or four instances of being bullied, you'll have plenty of ammunition for getting help. Remember, if the first adult you show your journal to doesn't help, keep showing it to other adults until someone does.

ABOUT THE AUTHOR

Jackie Humans knows firsthand what it's like to have a young child become the target of bullies and feel helpless to stop the bullying (her only child has Asperger Syndrome). Helping kids empower themselves is now her life's mission.

15 WAYS TO ZAP A BULLY!

For more information regarding Jackie Humans and her work, visit her website: www.jackiehumans.com.

Additional copies of this book may be purchased online from LegworkTeam.com, Amazon.com, BarnesandNoble.com, Borders.com, or via the author's website: www.jackiehumans.com.

You can also obtain a copy of the book by visiting L.I. Books or ordering it from your favorite bookstore.